IMAGES
of America

MOULTONBOROUGH

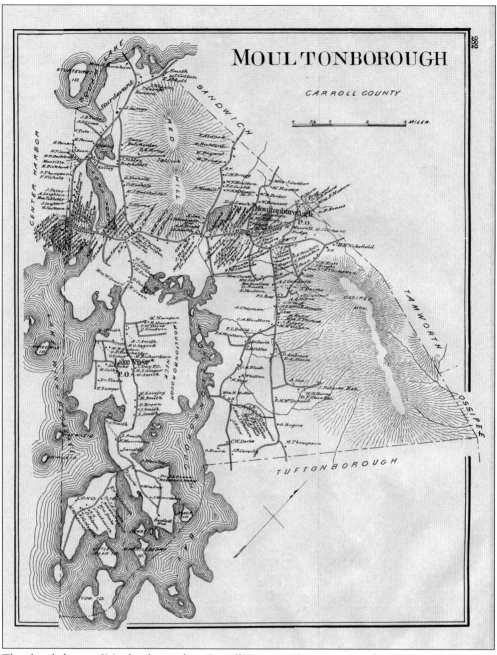

This detailed map of Moultonborough in Carroll County is from D.H. Hurd & Company's *Town and City Atlas of the State of New Hampshire*, which was published in Boston in 1892. (Moultonborough Historical Society.)

ON THE COVER: Often titled "The Square" on period postcards, this Main Street view of Moultonboro Corner taken around 1905 shows today's Moultonboro United Methodist Church to the left and the Old Country Store to the right. (Moultonborough Historical Society.)

IMAGES
of America

MOULTONBOROUGH

Cristina Ashjian and Jane Rice

ARCADIA
PUBLISHING

Published by Arcadia Publishing
Charleston, South Carolina

Printed in the United States of America

Library of Congress Control Number: 2023941838

For all general information, please contact Arcadia Publishing:
Telephone 843-853-2070
Fax 843-853-0044
E-mail sales@arcadiapublishing.com

Visit us on the Internet at www.arcadiapublishing.com

The Moultonborough Historical Society was organized in 1958 and incorporated in 1994 with the mission of preserving the past for the future. The Moultonborough History Museum is located in the historic Lamprey House, which is shown here. Known first as the Red Hill House and later as the Moultonboro Inn, this c. 1820 former boardinghouse was listed in the New Hampshire State Register of Historic Places in 2004. (Moultonborough Historical Society.)

CONTENTS

ACKNOWLEDGMENTS

We are grateful to the numerous people who helped make this book possible. Kathy Garry, president of the Moultonborough Historical Society, supported the project from its inception. All of the images are from the society's collection unless otherwise noted.

We are also grateful to the Camp Tecumseh Archives, Center Harbor Historical Society, Geneva Point Center Archives, Lake Winnipesaukee Historical Society and Museum, Laconia Public Library, Library of Congress, New Hampshire Historical Society, and Tuftonboro Historical Society for providing photographs from their collections.

We owe tremendous thanks to the many Moultonborough community members who contributed images from family albums to enrich our project. Our most difficult task was finalizing the image selection, since we received many more wonderful photographs than we were able to include in this publication. Special recognition is due to Dick Wakefield, whose extensive postcard collection frames the book's chapters. We have also benefited from the vast knowledge of and enthusiasm for our town's history as provided by key community members.

Historical information was taken from numerous sources, including published accounts, town reports, period maps, and talks given at Moultonborough Historical Society meetings. Most of these materials are available in the New Hampshire Room at the Moultonborough Public Library.

Aside from Moultonborough-specific materials, accounts of note include Georgia Drew Merrill's 1889 *History of Carroll County* (with the Moultonborough chapters written by W.H.H. Mason, MD) and Frank West Rollins's *The Tourists' Guide-Book to the State of New Hampshire* (1902, second edition), which was published by the Rumford Press in Concord. In addition, the 1908 *Town Register* published by the Mitchell-Cony Company in Augusta, Maine, provided valuable information about Moultonborough.

Special thanks are due to Eliza Tappé (for assistance with the detail maps found on each chapter title page) and Susan Weeks (for timely title research on key historic properties). We are grateful to the staff of the Moultonborough Public Library for providing us with meeting space throughout the project's duration. Finally, and above all, it is our hope that this book inspires further research into our town's unique history.

—Cristina Ashjian and Jane Rice

INTRODUCTION

Granted on November 17, 1763, and incorporated on November 24, 1777, Moultonborough was named in honor of Col. Jonathan Moulton. The first town meeting was held on March 31, 1778. The town's early population grew steadily and peaked in 1840, when it was recorded at 1,752. Following statewide trends, population declined after the Civil War and with the rise of urban industrialization, falling to 901 in 1900. In the late 19th century, there was an increase in farm abandonments, which led to local properties being advertised for sale in the New Hampshire Board of Agriculture's promotional *New Hampshire Farms for Summer Homes* publications.

Moultonborough's historical development is closely tied to its location between lakes and mountains, and to transportation routes established by the early 19th century. Surveyor Robert Fletcher's *Plan of Moultonborough* (1770) shows such defining landscape features as Red Hill, the Ossipee Mountains, Moultonborough Neck, Squam Lake, and Lake Winnipesaukee. The survey notes natural resources critical to the town's early mills and industries, including Red Hill Falls and Pond (now Garland Pond) and Long Pond (now Lake Kanasatka). J.R. Goodno's *Improved Reference and Distance Map of New Hampshire* (1833) identifies key stagecoach routes corresponding to today's Route 25 (Whittier Highway) and Route 109 (Governor Wentworth Highway). Whittier Highway remains the town's primary cultural roadway, with numerous historical resources along its length.

The town's early development patterns are best seen on E.M. Woodford's *Topographical Map of Carroll County, New Hampshire* (1861), and in D.H. Hurd's *Town and City Atlas of the State of New Hampshire* (1892), which feature private properties along with civic buildings, schools, and businesses. Along with historical accounts and early maps, period postcards provide valuable information and record ongoing changes to the town's streetscape and built environment. Despite rapid development over the past decades and significant losses over time, Moultonborough still has many structures, sites, and landscapes representing all periods of the town's history. These community assets define the town's unique character and cultural landscape.

The expansion of railway and steamboat lines in the late 19th century brought seasonal tourism to Moultonborough along with summer homes, country estates, and recreational facilities. The widely publicized Willey tragedy at Crawford Notch in 1826 marks the start of White Mountains tourism, and visitors keen to experience the primitive wilderness stopped over in the Lakes Region. Red Hill became a significant site for tourism in the mid-19th century with its close proximity to the port and hotels of Center Harbor. As seen in the *Calvert's Map of the Lakes Region* (1893), Moultonborough's Long Island (annexed on December 30, 1799) became an important transportation hub, allowing people and goods to be transported all over Lake Winnipesaukee. Long Island was Moultonborough's main port, and it was linked to the Boston & Maine Railroad line via the SS *Mount Washington*.

Period maps show how Moultonboro Corner (now Moultonborough Village), located at the intersection of stagecoach routes between area towns and lakeside landings, became the largest of the early settlements distributed throughout the town. Early commercial and industrial sites were located near Long Pond below Red Hill, where a sawmill was built on the main road. Moultonborough Centre (or Moultonborough Falls) at Sheridan Road was another early mill village, with industries on today's Garland Pond and the Red Hill River. In East Moultonborough, Lee's Mills on Lower Pond (now Lee's Pond) featured industrial and logging enterprises, and Three Bridges and Shannon Mills were located along today's Governor Wentworth Highway, which was built in 1771 as the College Road.

East Moultonborough was the earliest settled area in the town, and it remains the most rural in character. The Lee Settlement was established in the 1790s on the southern slopes of the Ossipee Mountains with links to valley farms and the earlier populated areas known as Birch Hill and Three Bridges. Publications from the 1840s focus on the natural and geologic attributes of the Ossipee range, noting the Cold Spring, Mineral Spring, and the waterfall (Ossipee Falls) located along Shannon Brook on lower elevations. Moultonborough's mineral water gained popularity and drew visitors seeking a cure for a host of maladies. This aspect of the town's early history has been eclipsed by the later transformations of the site by Benjamin Franklin Shaw and Thomas Gustave Plant in the late 19th and early 20th century.

Known for the scenic beauty of its lakes and mountains, rural Moultonborough experienced a surge in summer tourism in the late 19th century, as shown by the number of local accommodations listed in period guidebooks. M.F. Sweetser's *White Mountains: Handbook for Travellers* (1888) lists Moultonborough Bay, Moultonborough Neck, Long Island, and Ossipee Park (developed in the early 1880s) as destinations. Boardinghouses were located throughout the town along established coach routes, and many are listed in Frank West Rollins's *The Tourists' Guide-Book to the State of New Hampshire*. Several boardinghouses survive today along the Route 25 corridor, including Maple Cottage by Lake Kanasatka, the New Cambridge House and Red Hill Cottage (later Fairmont) at Green's Corner, and Oakland House, the Red Hill House (later Moultonboro Inn), Maplehurst, and Hillcrest Farm in today's Moultonborough Village.

Improvements in transportation around Lake Winnipesaukee resulted in summer tourism as well as the building of grand country estates. The Greene brothers developed notable estates (Roxmont and Windermere) near the Long Island Inn and landing in the early 1890s, along with the Roxmont Poultry Farm on Moultonborough Neck. Exemplifying the strategy promoted by *New Hampshire Farms for Summer Homes*, Herbert Dumaresq bought a number of farms in 1899 and built his splendid country estate, known as Kona Farm, on Moultonborough Neck starting in 1900. Thomas Sheridan's agricultural estate near Red Hill was developed after 1903. Making the former Ossipee Mountain Park the centerpiece of his country estate, Thomas Plant constructed Lucknow (now the Castle in the Clouds) in East Moultonborough in 1913–1914.

With its temperate climate, Moultonborough Neck played an agricultural role in early town history. By 1900, boardinghouse and summer home tourism were significant to the area's development. Green's Basin was a popular tourist destination featured in numerous postcards documenting boating and other recreational activities. Originally established as the Geneva Point Camp on the Roxmont Poultry Farm (and later Winnipesaukee Inn) property, the Geneva Point Center celebrated its centennial in 2019. The Neck became a site for youth summer camps in the early 20th century, and three of these lakefront camps still exist: Camp Tecumseh (established in 1903), Camp Winaukee (established in 1920), and Camp Robindel (established in 1951). Many other early camps have been redeveloped into summer home properties.

The course of the 20th century saw numerous summer homes and residential colonies established throughout Moultonborough. Thomas Plant developed today's Bald Peak Colony Club on his lakefront property starting in 1919, and the centennial of its opening was celebrated in 2021. Elsewhere in town, the expansion of automobile routes and the advent of middle-class tourism resulted in the construction of gas stations and other facilities for motorists, such as the Red Hill Restaurant and Camps on Whittier Highway, which was established in 1935. The historic steamboat landing at Lee's Mills, which is now home to town docks, has been the site of the annual Lee's Mills Steamboat Meet since 1972. By the 1950s, Moultonborough's early agricultural economy had completed its transformation into the tourism and services economy that remains today.

One

MOULTONBOROUGH

VILLAGE

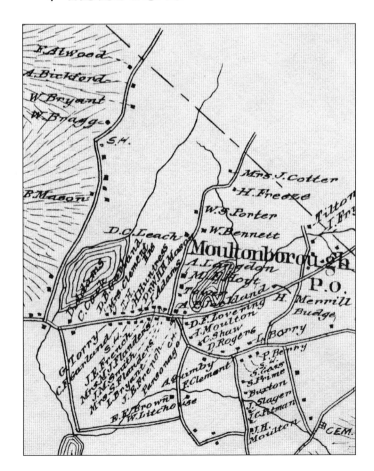

This detail showing Moultonboro Corner or Moultonborough post office is taken from D.H. Hurd's *Town and City Atlas of the State of New Hampshire* (1892).

This c. 1925 photograph of Moultonboro Corner was taken from the hillside where the Methodist parsonage once stood next to the Moultonborough Public Library. The image shows part of the portico on the Richardson Grain Store (which burned down in 1994) next to the Moultonboro Methodist Church at left, and Alfred Freese's Maplehurst boardinghouse and store beyond today's Old Country Store to the right. (Dick Wakefield Collection.)

Built by the Second Congregational Meeting House Assoociation in 1851–1852, and originally located next to the Moultonborough Town House, the church was sold to the Methodists in 1869 and moved to its present location. This c. 1925 view shows how the slope allowed for the addition of a basement-level vestry. James French donated the bell in 1884, and the stained-glass windows, dedicated to French and others, were installed in 1905–1906.

10

The Old Country Store, which was listed in the National Register of Historic Places in 1982 as Freese's Tavern, has housed a general store, a tavern, offices, library rooms, and a post office over the years. Built in 1781, this landmark at Moultonboro Corner is located at the historic crossroads for stagecoach routes. In this c. 1905 image, a Concord Coach is shown in front of what was then George Richardson's store. (Holden family.)

This c. 1920 image, taken in front of the Moultonboro Methodist Church near the village well and bandstand, shows the gable end of the Methodist parsonage situated on the hill across the corner intersection. Eliza True willed her property to the Methodist church upon her death in 1880 for use as a parsonage, and the house and its outbuildings were demolished around 1991. (Dick Wakefield Collection.)

This c. 1915 postcard view of Main Street shows the new Knights of Pythias Hall built in 1914 for Chocorua Lodge No. 164. The hall was used for community events including suppers, dances, school graduations, and movie screenings. The Knights of Pythias Hall was sold in 1967 and demolished in 1971 after the brick Clyde Foss insurance agency building was constructed next door. (Dick Wakefield Collection.)

This view farther down Main Street dates to around 1915 and shows Moultonboro Corner with Alfred Freese's Maplehurst boardinghouse at left (behind the row of trees) and the Moultonboro Methodist Church at right. The general store's porch is visible at center left, with George Blanchard's Homestead boardinghouse just beyond it, and the Methodist parsonage on the knoll at the center of the image. (Dick Wakefield Collection.)

Moultonboro Corner's original school (District No. 3) was located on Main Street across from the Moultonboro Town House and the Lamprey House. Used until 1925, this building was replaced by the Village School, which was constructed in 1926 near the present-day intersection of Old Route 109 and Whittier Highway, and later used as the New Hampshire State Police barracks. All of the district schools were closed when Moultonborough Central School opened in 1949.

Alfred Freese's Maplehurst accommodated 10 guests at $1 per day and was described in Frank West Rollins's *The Tourists' Guide-Book to the State of New Hampshire* (1902) as "situated in centre of village near telephone, post-office, and church. House open to transients the year round." As shown here, Freese also operated the store next door (formerly run by Flanders, then by Perkins in the 1920s), which later became Tilton's Store. (Scott Lamprey.)

The Moultonborough Grange No. 197 purchased the Red Hill House, a former tavern, in 1894, and the structure had been substantially renovated by 1904. The interior exhibits features characteristic of a Grange Hall, including an upstairs auditorium. Built around 1810 and photographed in May 1929, the Moultonborough Grange Hall was listed in the New Hampshire State Register of Historic Places and added to the statewide Seven to Save endangered property list in 2012.

The Town of Moultonborough celebrated the nation's bicentennial in 1976 with three days of events on July 30, July 31, and August 1. A street parade was held on July 31, followed by a bean supper at the Moultonboro United Methodist Church and a street dance in the village. Here, a float with Grange members, town officials, and state representatives awaits the start of the parade in front of the Moultonborough Grange Hall.

The Moultonborough Town House was built in 1834–1835 and used for March town meetings from 1835 through 1949. Prior to the construction of the Town House, town meetings were held in meetinghouses and other local locations. The vernacular Town House, listed in the National Register of Historic Places in 1989 and the State Register in 2004, was also used for Congregational religious services until around 1852. (Oliver family.)

On August 25, 1946, Moultonborough dedicated a memorial to those who served in the armed forces during World War II. Here, Sen. Styles Bridges is at the Town House addressing the crowd. The tablet inset in a boulder and the honor roll to the right of the Town House doors were unveiled at this event, with music provided by the Center Harbor Band. (George Lamprey.)

Built around 1820, the Federal-style Emerson-Mohr House was owned by the Hon. Samuel Emerson in 1861 and by Isaac Adams in 1892. Later run by Isaac Moulton as the Oakland House, it was described in Frank West Rollins's *The Tourists' Guide-Book to the State of New Hampshire* (1902) as "pleasantly located with piazza, shade trees and oak grove. Good fishing ground near. Within two minutes' walk of post-office and telephone." It accommodated 20 guests for $1 per day.

Built around 1853, this Gothic Revival house was the home of Dr. W.H.H. Mason, a physician, landowner, and author of the Moultonborough chapters in the 1889 *History of Carroll County*. In this photograph from the 1924 Grange Fair parade, state representative and town official George Blanchard is walking in front of what was then the Richardson house, while his granddaughter Adele Ambrose (later Taylor) follows on horseback.

The French house, formerly located across from the Grange Hall at the village center, was the home of prominent state legislator, town official, and businessman James E. "Jim" French until his death in 1919. French also owned the general store previously operated by his father. James French enlarged the c. 1840 broad gabled house shown in this c. 1880 stereograph by adding a second floor around 1900. (Dick Plaisted.)

After the Homestead burned in 1923, George Blanchard moved his family into the French house, shown here in April 1925. Blanchard's granddaughter Adele Taylor, Moultonborough's longest-serving librarian (47 years), was the property's last resident. The French-Taylor House was listed in the New Hampshire State Register of Historic Places in 2017 and added to the New Hampshire Preservation Alliance's Seven to Save endangered property list that same year. This landmark was demolished by the Town of Moultonborough in 2021.

This c. 1880 stereograph of Augustus Jaclard's boardinghouse and Union Hall shows the property from across the street near the Old Country Store. Union Hall, where community and Grange meetings took place in the 1890s, was included in the State of New Hampshire's 1890 list of boarding establishments. Augustus Jaclard's daughter Adele married grain merchant George Blanchard, and they operated her family's property as the Homestead in the early 20th century.

Advertised as "a charming home-like place to find rest and comfort" located in a "small village" and "connected with the outside world by local and long distance telephone," the Homestead at Moultonboro Corner accommodated 20 guests at $1.50 per day year-round. A chimney fire destroyed the property in February 1923. Here, participants in the 1922 Grange Fair parade pass by the Homestead on Main Street.

Hillcrest Farm on Holland Street, now known as the Holland Hill House, was one of Moultonboro Corner's several boarding establishments. Proprietors Henry and Mabel Boyle, who also owned Hillcrest Tavern, rented rooms into the 1940s. The farm's former dairy barn, now a residence, is directly across the street. The carriage shed previously on site was demolished around 2015. (Dick Wakefield Collection.)

Berry Pond was a recreational site for tourists. The Homestead's brochure promoted this "very picturesque pond within three minutes' walk of house." The 1908 *Town Register* notes, "Little Winnipesaukee is a beautiful sheet of water near Moultonboro Corner, containing about 200 acres. Many kinds of fish abound here, and in the hunting season it is a popular place with the sportsmen." (Dick Wakefield Collection.)

The Moultonborough Public Library was constructed in 1929 with funds bequeathed by James E. French upon his death in 1919 "for the purpose of building a library building at Moultonborough Corner." French's widow, Martha H., conveyed the building site to the town in 1923. A bronze plaque inside honors French, a library trustee from 1897 to 1917, "who for many years spared no effort on behalf of the town." (Dick Wakefield Collection.)

By the mid-1830s, Moultonboro Corner, located at the intersection of stagecoach routes between area towns and lake landings, had developed into the municipal center it remains. This c. 1930 view looking east along Main Street shows Tilton's Store & Lunch Room at left, today's Old Country Store (formerly Freese's Tavern) at center, and the newly built public library at right. (Dick Wakefield Collection.)

This c. 1930 image shows the Moultonborough Grange Hall and the Knights of Pythias Hall, both centers of community activity, side by side on Moultonboro Corner's Main Street. In its statistics, the 1908 *Town Register* notes that there were 75 members each in the Moultonborough Grange No. 197 and the Knights of Pythias Chocorua Lodge No. 164 in that census year, with an estimated town population of 975. (Dick Wakefield Collection.)

This c. 1930 image shows the view looking toward the Ossipee Mountains from Moultonboro Corner, with the Ralph Goodwin family bungalow (constructed in 1926) at right. The Dr. Frank Lovering house, which was sold out of that family in 1932 and later operated as a boardinghouse known as Hillcrest Tavern, is visible at center through the trees. (Dick Wakefield Collection.)

The Bartlett House (above), with its village barn, was located on Holland Street just beyond the present-day location of the Old Country Store. It was demolished in 2006 with a controlled burn to create a parking lot. (Dick Wakefield Collection.)

The Moses E. Hoyt House, which was also destroyed by fire, was farther up Holland Street on the road to Center Sandwich. Hoyt and his two sons Charles and Jones are listed as carpenters in the 1908 *Town Register.* (Dick Wakefield Collection.)

The Country Fare Inn, which formerly stood at the corner of Route 25 and Old Route 109, was built as Moultonborough's first Methodist church and remained in use from 1843 to 1869. The building was sold in 1883 and converted to a residence, and later housed the medical practice of Dr. Frank Judkins. (Dick Wakefield Collection.)

Dr. Judkins sold his home and practice to Dr. Frank Lovering in 1891, and the Lovering family owned the former church until 1932. These postcards show the property in the 1960s, when it was operated by Kenneth Smith as the Country Fare Inn. This landmark was demolished in 2017. (Dick Wakefield Collection.)

The Moultonborough Volunteer Fire Department formed in 1932, and the firehouse shown here was built in 1933 on land donated by Paul Blanchard. This July 1934 photograph shows, from left to right, (first row) Robert Lamprey (chief), Ralph Morrill, John Randall, Harold Frye, Paul Blanchard, and Walter Rollo; (second row) Harvey Moulton, Burleigh Moulton, Ralph Goodwin, Richard Moulton, Fred Stevens, and Lisle Davis. The building is now used for storage.

The Hi There Café, opened by Leila and George Gillooly around 1959, was a local diner known for its fried dough dipped in maple syrup and free ice cream for children who marched in the Fourth of July parade. Later known as the Hi There Restaurant and operated by Art and Natalie Lively from 1971 to 1982, it was more recently home to the Chowder Barn and Artie's Subs and Pizza. (Dick Wakefield Collection.)

Two

WEST SIDE

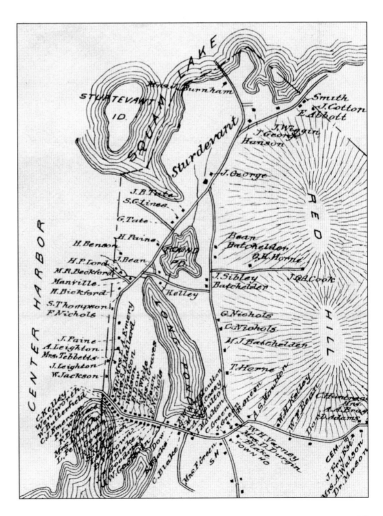

This detail showing the Center Harbor town line to Green's Corner is taken from D.H. Hurd's 1892 *Town and City Atlas of the State of New Hampshire*.

Built as a Universalist church, this building stood near the Center Harbor town line. Used as a school in the early 20th century, it later housed a dance hall, a roller-skating rink, and other commercial enterprises before it was demolished in 1965 to make way for Lee Huston's Texaco gas station.

The former Center Harbor Garage still stands near the town line across from Bean Road. Originally the Neal-Wentworth boat-building and blacksmith shop, this gable-front building later housed the Center Harbor post office (from 1957 to 1970), the Alvord Pharmacy, and the Di Salvo PA offices until it was converted for residential use.

Situated on Bean Road just past Kelsea Avenue, the Pines was a boardinghouse operated by Florence Goudey in the 1930s. An earlier postcard showing golfers putting on the lawn outside the house identifies the property as the Winnipesaukee Country Club. More recently, the house has been used as a church for various congregations. (Author's collection.)

Grove Hill Farm, one of the original Bean family homesteads, operated as a seasonal boardinghouse in the early 20th century. Accommodating 14 guests at $1.25 per day, it was described in Frank West Rollins's *The Tourists' Guide-Book to the State of New Hampshire* (1902) as "Situated 15 minutes' walk from Centre Harbor post-office, church and steamboat landing, in pleasant location, easy of access," with "good country board." (Dick Wakefield Collection.)

The Bean Road School, shown here in a dilapidated state around 1890, stood near the intersection of Bean and Sibley Roads just north of Lake Kanasatka. According to Frances Stevens's memoirs, which were published in 1987, the school was moved at least twice and rebuilt into a residence after its use as a school was discontinued. (Roger Kelley Collection, Center Harbor Historical Society.)

Kent Island, Squam Lake, near Center Harbor, N. H.

Shown here from Bean Road near the Sandwich town line, Kent Island was acquired by John and Sarah Cook for $70 in 1886. The descendants of their son Asa Sinclair Cook still populate Kent Island in the summer months. The Cooks were one of the earliest families to establish rustic camps on Squam Lake's islands. (Dick Wakefield Collection.)

Originally owned by John Cotton, this Bean Road farm became a summer property in 1919, exemplifying the *New Hampshire Farms for Summer Homes* initiative promoted in the early 20th century. This image of the barnyard with Ernest Stevens and Ernest Daigneau at work dates to 1947, when the farm was owned by Theodore Brown. (Lisa Wardlaw.)

Dating to 1937, this photograph was taken when a house was being built on the hillside overlooking Cotton Farm, Kent Island, and the Squam range. Family albums from the 1930s onward show ongoing farming, along with boating on the lake and other recreational activities of what was known as the Cotton Farm Colony. (Lisa Wardlaw.)

Still known as "The Shanty" by the Cook family, this rustic fishing camp on Kent Island was built in 1887 by Asa Sinclair Cook and his brother J. Otis Cook. The red canoe (covered here) was 18 feet long, and it appears in a number of early photographs taken on Squam Lake. (Jarvis family.)

Patriarch Asa Sinclair Cook is seated in the bow of the rowboat in this photograph. The Cook brothers (Asa and J. Otis) and their friends, including members of the Pratt family (who would later establish seasonal camps on Brown Point), fished on Squam Lake year-round. (Jarvis family.)

Asa Sinclair Cook had a big cottage built on Kent Island in 1888, and over time, additional cottages were added to the Cook family compound. Cook was included in the list of seasonal residents published in the 1904 edition of *New Hampshire Farms for Summer Homes*. (Jarvis family.)

Images in family albums document updates to the Cook family cottages, and most island work was done over the winter, when supplies were transported over the ice. The Jarvis house was renovated in 1914, and its boathouse (with sundeck) was built in the 1940s. (Jarvis family.)

Dr. Ann Tomkins Gibson, known as Doc Ann, was the director of Singing Eagle Lodge, a two-month-long girls' camp in operation on Squam Lake from 1922 to 1966. Campers slept in platform tents along the shoreline and engaged in numerous activities, including a modern dance program in the 1930s. (Singing Eagle Lodge.)

The historic Singing Eagle Lodge property's waterfront featured an unobstructed view of East Rattlesnake and the Squam range. In 1975, a group of alumnae successfully reopened the camp as a two-week enterprise; this continues to operate at Camp Deerwood in Holderness. (Singing Eagle Lodge.)

Initially accommodating 40 boys, Camp Quinebarge was founded in 1936 by Henry C. Kenly, who enlisted older campers in the camp's early years to build cabins on the 75-acre property along Lake Kanasatka's shoreline. Campers also built floats to participate in Center Harbor's annual Fourth of July parade. (Camp Quinebarge.)

Tom and Barbara Brunelle acquired Camp Quinebarge in 1962, expanding its capacity and introducing a riding program. The camp, which has been coeducational since 1975, is still in operation today, with meetings, campfires, and cookouts held at Piney Point overlooking Lake Kanasatka. (Camp Quinebarge.)

The Oak Corner House was located along today's Lake Shore Drive at Alpine Park Road. Whittier Highway, the main road between Moultonborough and Center Harbor, was widened and rerouted in 1954, bypassing what is now Lake Shore Drive. (Dick Wakefield Collection.)

Operated by Angelina Amabile and family, the Oak Corner House was run as a summer inn with cottages from the 1920s into the 1950s, with docks and a beach on Center Harbor Bay. (Dick Wakefield Collection.)

Cluster Cove, run by the Goodrich family in the early 20th century and since demolished, was a boardinghouse at the west end of today's Lake Shore Drive opposite Lake Kanasatka. (Dick Wakefield Collection.)

These c. 1910 postcards show the roadway along what was then Long Pond with a view to Red Hill and the mill behind Cluster Cove, which was also owned and operated by the Goodrich family. (Dick Wakefield Collection.)

The Goodrich Mill, shown here around 1895, was located on the main road opposite the dam at Long Pond. Percy Kelley operated the mill in the early 20th century, and he introduced electricity generated at the mill to Center Harbor in 1910. The mill was destroyed by fire around 1937. (New Hampshire Historical Society.)

This hillside view from near Glidden Road, formerly known as Jack Road, shows the millhouse and expanded grist- and sawmill buildings at the outlet of Long Pond, and area farms and open fields going up the hill to what is now known as Birch Lane. (Roger Kelley Collection, Center Harbor Historical Society.)

This photograph of the Goodrich Mill and Mill Corner at Long Pond, taken from the west side, shows the millhouse in an early state around 1900, before the wide porch (visible in later images) was added to its front elevation. (Leach family.)

This later image of the millhouse shows the house before the addition of dormers that are on the house today. The property is locally called the Red Mill House and was most recently known as Conway's Bait Shop. (Lake Winnipesaukee Historical Society.)

Camp Vonhurst, established as a camp for "adults and their families" by Frederick H. von der Sump around 1930, featured a main lodge and cottages in the woods on 60 acres along Lake Kanasatka's shoreline. Guests enjoyed activities including fishing, swimming, and hiking, as well as fish frys and beach parties. (Peter Lawlor.)

In August 1933, a Mr. Daigneau, along with his team of oxen, cleared Camp Vonhurst's beach. There is a series of photographs taken by Charlie Brady showing the oxen dragging stones off the rocky shoreline. Here, the camp's proprietor, known as Von, sits astride the ox to the left, while Camp Vonhurst guests look on. (Peter Lawlor.)

Maple Cottage was listed in Frank West Rollins's *The Tourists' Guide-Book to the State of New Hampshire* (1902) when it was being operated as a boardinghouse by Alvin Moulton around 1900. Run by Moulton's daughter Hattie with her husband, Myron Fletcher, starting in the 1910s, the property now known as Maple Cottages sits directly across from Redding Lane above Lake Kanasatka. (Dick Wakefield Collection.)

This c. 1930 photograph, taken from Whittier Highway, shows the undeveloped Lake Kanasatka shoreline. Prior to the advent of summer tourism, Long Pond was known for its logging and mill enterprises, as depicted in the W.H. Bartlett engraving *Saw Mill at Centre Harbor*, published in *American Scenery* in 1840. (Dick Wakefield Collection.)

The Hanson Farm, located on Moultonborough's Second Neck, was run as a seasonal boardinghouse by Rufus and Mary Hanson and, later, their son Charles. Hanson family members are shown standing in front of their farmhouse around 1903, with summer boarders seated on the steps to the right.

Boardinghouse guests enjoyed Hanson Farm produce and area recreational activities, as indicated by the group of boarders with tennis racquets shown here. After the Hanson farmhouse was demolished, the greater farm property was sold and developed into Krainewood Shores by Peter Kraines in the mid-1960s.

Starting in the 1940s, the Labombarde family summered on Moultonborough's Second Neck at a camp compound built on the tree-lined shoreline of the Hanson Farm. The family camp was sold in 2016 and subsequently demolished. (Peter Labombarde.)

Camp life included boating on the family's 42-foot Wheeler yacht *Halcyon* and collecting water at the Redding Lane Spring. Phil Labombarde flew to and from Lake Winnipesaukee on his Grumman G-44 Widgeon amphibious airplane. (Peter Labombarde.)

This view looking toward Green's Corner shows the Moulton-Greene-Leach House with its connected barns at the crest of the hill. Built around 1840 by Samuel Moulton, the farm was acquired by Charles Greene in 1882 and is still used as a seasonal property by his descendants. The Greek Revival farmhouse was listed in the New Hampshire State Register of Historic Places in 2009. (Leach family.)

Huston's gas station, pictured in 1945, was located at the corner of Moultonborough Neck Road and Whittier Highway. The property became the Kracker Box convenience store in the 1960s, when it was run by Louis Moscardini. The Kracker Box sign is now in the collection of Moultonborough Historical Society. (Mary Smith Collection.)

A Picnic Party at Green's Basin, Lake Winnipesaukee, N. H.

Green's Basin was a popular recreational site frequented by guests staying at area boardinghouses. Robert Greene, then a college student, built a fishing camp on a cliff overlooking Tea Rock in 1908, which is one of the oldest camps still on the Basin. Robert's nephew Rev. Frank E. Greene, a poet and scholar, wrote *Uncle Bob's Camp: Poems of a Place* (1983) as a tribute to his late uncle. (Dick Wakefield Collection.)

The William Plant family, whose Camp Tanglewood was on Tuftonboro Neck, made day trips and overnight excursions on the *Margaret V*, shown here in Green's Basin in August 1912. William Plant's daughter Amy and sons Bill, Tom, and Everett were close to their uncle Thomas Plant, who built his country estate Lucknow (now the Castle in the Clouds) in the Ossipees in 1914. (Plant family.)

Mrs. Frank Green was the proprietor of the Red Hill Cottage in 1890, when it was included in the New Hampshire Board of Agriculture's list of boarding establishments. The house still stands and is located behind the gas station across from the Moulton-Greene-Leach House at Green's Corner. (New Hampshire Historical Society.)

The former Red Hill Cottage boardinghouse, shown here on a postcard, was later known as Fairmont and is listed in Frank West Rollins's *The Tourists' Guide-Book to the State of New Hampshire* (1902) as being operated by a Mrs. Ames. On the 1892 map, it appears north of the Green's Corner School at the top of Moultonborough Neck and was operated by Mrs. Frank Green.

Rolland Green of Cambridge, Massachusetts, acquired 130 acres of farmland on the hillside overlooking Long Pond in 1881, then built and operated the Cambridge House as a seasonal boarding enterprise until it burned down around 1900. Mattie Mason, sister of his wife, Nancy, was an artist and art instructor, and a number of her works are in local collections. (New Hampshire Historical Society.)

The New Cambridge House, built in 1900 to replace the Cambridge House, stands on Ames Road near Green's Corner. The house, connected to a large gambrel barn, features a mansard roof in the French Second Empire style. In Frank West Rollins's *The Tourists' Guide-Book to the State of New Hampshire* (1902), the property is listed as being operated by Rolland Green; it was operated by his nephew Fred Ames and family into the 1940s. (Leach family.)

Wallace Greene Arnold established the Toltecs camp for boys in Weston, Connecticut, then moved it to Charlestown, New Hampshire, in 1949. Toltec Lodge on Lake Winnipesaukee, which gives Toltec Point its name, was offered as "an outpost camp where boys experience primitive living for a part of each summer." Toltecs boys spent two or more weeks at Lake Winnipesaukee, where they enjoyed water sports and shared work with their counselors on a wooded parcel with a mile of shorefront, a beach, and a sheltered cove. The 140-acre Toltecs property was sold and developed into Arcadia Campground in the 1960s. (Hilton family.)

Three

RED HILL AND MOULTONBOROUGH FALLS

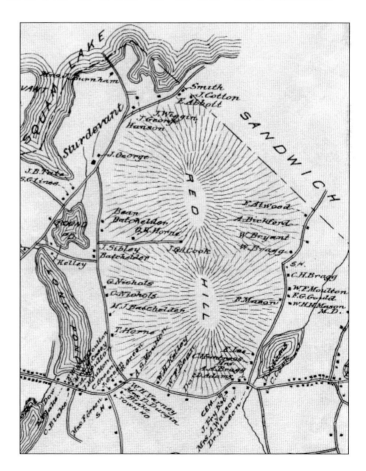

This detail showing Red Hill and Moultonboro Falls to the Sandwich town line is taken from D.H. Hurd's 1892 *Town and City Atlas of the State of New Hampshire*.

After it was acquired by Chester Davis in 1919, the Varney homestead, shown here in 1918, was enlarged and updated as the Davis Farm expanded its operations. Chet Davis's sawmill, which gives Sawmill Way its name, was active for over 40 years and was most recently run by Ron and Rae Marie Davis. (Davis family.)

Sunny Farm, formerly the Thomas Horne property, still stands on Red Hill Road. The Horne farm is noted both on the 1861 and 1892 town maps. In the 1942 real estate assessment list, this 200-acre farm was owned by Freeman Horne's widow, Ella, and valued at $1,500. (Lake Winnipesaukee Historical Society.)

The historic Sturtevant and Sibley farms are located in the valley below Red Hill between Lake Kanasatka and Wakondah Pond. The Sibley farmhouse, said to be built around the Israel Glines log cabin (which dates to around 1775), is one of the oldest in town, and it is still inhabited by Sturtevant descendants. (Cynthia Carver.)

Lewis Sibley, a stonemason from Somerville, Massachusetts, moved to Center Harbor to work at the Sutton Farm in the early 1870s and married Ella Sturtevant in 1877, moving to her family's farm property. He built the Sibley Fountain, which still stands at the corner of Sibley and Red Hill Roads. (Dick Wakefield Collection.)

Having attended the Toltecs camp (later working as a counselor there), Ted Hilton established the Plumfield Camp for Boys in 1948, changing its name to Deer Hill Camp in 1953. Deer Hill operated at his hillside property on Red Hill Road and Lake Kanasatka until 2003. (Hilton family.)

Boys attending Deer Hill Camp, which promoted a flexible individualized program, also spent time in the White Mountains at a log cabin in Warren. Period brochures define the camp's mission to teach fundamental skills and build confidence. The camp became coeducational in 1986. (Hilton family.)

In 1952, Ted Hilton acquired the historic Batchelder farm property on Lake Kanasatka, which had been the summer home of the Hotchkiss family into the 1940s. Many former farms became summer camps in the early 20th century, and most of them have since been subdivided and developed. (Hilton family.)

This image of Deer Hill Camp's waterfront in the 1950s shows how Lake Kanasatka remained mostly undeveloped in the camp's early days. However, with development pressures increasing in the 1960s, Ted Hilton founded the Lake Kanasatka Watershed Association in 1972. (Hilton family.)

The Red Hill fire tower, first manned in 1927, was built to replace an earlier fire lookout on Mount Israel. Funds to build the tower and cabin were donated by Ernest B. Dane of Center Harbor. The Lakes Region Conservation Trust maintains the popular hiking trail that leads to the summit of Red Hill. (Hilton family.)

The site of the Ebenezer Horne house, which is now just a cellar hole, is located along the hiking trail to the summit of Red Hill. Built about 1828, the Horne house was abandoned after 1898 and torn down after a lost cow from the Dane Farm in Center Harbor was discovered trapped in its ruins. (Library of Congress.)

Red Hill was a popular destination for tourists as early as 1833, and its panoramic view was celebrated in the W.H. Bartlett engraving *Lake Winnipisseogee from Red Hill*, published in *American Scenery* in 1840. Bartlett, who stayed at the Senter House in Center Harbor, climbed "Red Mountain" in August 1836. (Dick Wakefield Collection.)

Jonathan Cook, a Revolutionary War veteran, and his wife, Charlotte, lived on Red Hill in the "saddle" between the two summits. The Cooks kept a visitors' book starting in 1833, and it was signed by tourists who ascended Red Hill, including Franklin Pierce, Daniel Webster, Ralph Waldo Emerson, and many others. (Dick Wakefield Collection.)

Harry and Eurie Richardson acquired the historic Bean property in 1901, which is said to be where Major Bean conducted militia training for the Revolutionary War. The Cape farmhouse, now Casual Cape, still stands, but the barn and outbuildings shown in this image of Harry Richardson working on his farm are long gone. (Richardson family.)

With increased automobile traffic passing by his farm on Whittier Highway, Harry Richardson converted an outbuilding next to his large barn into a Red Top store and Socony gas station. All of the buildings shown here, along with 20 tons of hay, were destroyed by a massive fire and explosion on August 25, 1938. (Richardson family.)

Working with crosscut saws, axes, and horse-drawn sleds, the Richardson family salvaged timber from trees brought down on Moultonborough Neck by the hurricane of 1938. The lumber was milled at the nearby Chet Davis sawmill and used to build a new gambrel barn, shown here under construction in early 1939. (Richardson family.)

Harry Richardson's replacement barn was completed in 1939 and featured a stone silo toward the rear of the structure. The silo was later removed, and doors and a shed dormer now fill its space. This massive structure still stands on Whittier Highway, where it now houses Goodhue Marine and Firearms. (Richardson family.)

The Red Hill Restaurant, constructed with salvaged timber after the hurricane of 1938, was built next to the Richardson farmhouse on Whittier Highway. Initially known as the Red Hill Restaurant, it later became Ben's Steak House, then the Blink Bonnie Scottish shop and other commercial ventures. (Dick Wakefield Collection.)

Harry Richardson built several overnight cottages for tourists to meet the demands of automobile tourism in the 1930s. His sister-in-law Ethel Smith's diary reports that the Red Hill Camps were built in July 1935 and were so popular that the family had to turn "hundreds" away on the Fourth of July in 1936. (Dick Wakefield Collection.)

Moultonborough Centre (or Moultonborough Falls) was a mill village with early industries on Garland Pond and the Red Hill River. Durwand Adams owned the sawmill in 1889, and this postcard photograph, taken from the bridge, shows the Adams house, with its two-story open porch on the right, prior to demolition in the late 1960s.

This view of Moultonborough Falls and Red Hill, printed from a glass negative, includes the Bragg family houses at right (after the turn to Sheridan Road), and the Mason, Watson, and Fry properties on the left side of the main road. In 1889, the gristmill was owned by the Mason family, who also had farms on Sheridan Road.

Joseph Meloon, who worked in insurance, built a new house at Moultonborough Falls in 1899. This image, printed from a glass negative, was taken from the Sheridan Road side of the property and shows the house under construction. The gristmill at the Falls, which was demolished in the mid-1960s, is visible across the main road.

This image of the Joseph Meloon house, also printed from a glass negative, shows the house situated at the corner of Sheridan Road and Whittier Highway, much as it appears today. A later image of Joseph and Elizabeth Meloon enjoying a double glider swing in their garden also reveals the open pastures and stone walls along Sheridan Road.

The Henry Grant blacksmith shop at Moultonborough Falls was listed in the *New Hampshire Register* business directory of 1906–1907. Blacksmith shops were located throughout the town and recorded on the 1861 map along with other early industries. Grant appears in photographs taken at the Falls around 1900.

Established by Jonathan Moulton in 1765, the Moultonborough Falls mill complex (a dam, gristmills, and sawmills) is a significant industrial archaeological resource. This postcard shows the old dam on the north side of the bridge on Whittier Highway. The left side of the breached dam collapsed around 2016. (Dick Wakefield Collection.)

This photograph of the Lee farmhouse and barn, printed from a glass negative, was taken in July 1899. Descendants of this early Moultonborough family, best known for its long tenure at the Lee Settlement (established on Ossipee Mountain in the early 1760s), still inhabit the Sheridan Road property, which is now known as the Oliver Farm.

Taken at the Lee Farm on Sheridan Road, this 1942 photograph shows Lizzie Lee Porter with her calf outside the barn. Photographs from family albums record the acquisition of a farm truck in 1931, expansion of the farmhouse in the mid-1930s, and diversified farming well into the 1940s. (Oliver family.)

Thomas Sheridan of Chicago acquired the historic Mason farm in 1903, developing his Red Hill Farm into a country estate complete with a large barn and numerous outbuildings. The 800-acre farm was featured in the 1911 edition of *New Hampshire Farms for Summer Homes*. (Follett family.)

Images from the early 1950s show agricultural outbuildings adjacent to the large barn compound, with its two silos, that still stands on Sheridan Road. Farm buildings included a calf barn, pig house, blacksmith shop, garage, and the brooder house and poultry barn along Buxton Road. (Follett family.)

In 1890, Frank and Emma Atwood bought a farm near the Sandwich town line, and what is now known as Abbott Farm remains in the family and is now farmed by a fifth generation. In the 1920s, Arthur Abbott sold 100 acres of land to buy a team of draft horses, shown here outside the barn. (Abbott family.)

Taken in the driveway outside the Tilton house on Sheridan Road, this photograph shows Carroll County deputy sheriff Chucky Severance at left, with Harold Tilton, who was the Moultonborough Police chief in the mid-1960s. The poultry barn on the Sheridan farm is visible in the valley beyond. (Don Muscavitz Jr.)

Four

MOULTONBOROUGH NECK

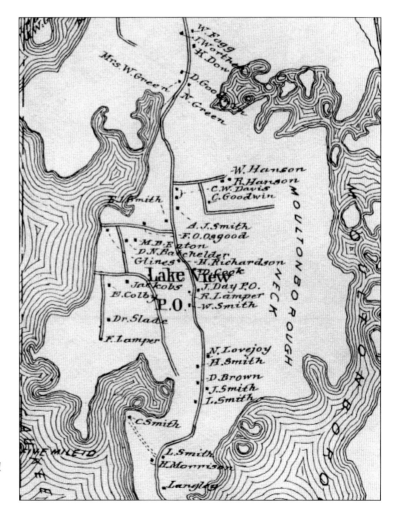

This detail showing Moultonborough Neck with the Lake View post office is taken from D.H. Hurd's 1892 *Town and City Atlas of the State of New Hampshire.*

Nathan Greene came to Moultonborough in 1802 and built a two-room house where he and his wife, Sarah, raised nine children. In 1816, known as the "year without summer," their son Jonathan started to build his own house on a snowy June day, according to family lore. Jonathan Greene's Federal-style house, completed around 1819, still stands on Moultonborough Neck Road. (Gruner family.)

This view of the prosperous Greene farm around 1900 shows an extensive connected farm compound with multiple sheds and barns, indicating industries other than farming. Later known as Green Bay Lodge, the property was owned and operated by Olga K. Gruner as a summer guesthouse between 1947 and 1977. The business included six rental cottages at Green's Basin. (Gruner family.)

In 1946, Alan and Jessie "Jep" Davisson acquired the historic 100-acre Abbott Farm from Louis Hastings, who had owned what was called Rough Beach Farm since 1918. Summer residents of the Far Echoes Colony since the 1920s, the Davissons moved to Moultonborough Neck full-time, and their son Al farmed the property for decades, also operating Davisson Farm Enterprises. (Mark Dodd.)

This view of the Davisson Farm shows a number of outbuildings connecting the Cape farmhouse to a large barn, the characteristic configuration unique to northern New England. Al Davisson was an avid farmer and orchardist, as shown in the many photographs of his activities in family albums. The farm was sold by the family in 2019, and the farm's barn underwent a major restoration in 2022. (Mark Dodd.)

Orchard Farm is located at the crest of Moultonborough Neck and features expansive views of the Ossipee Mountains. A warranty deed dating to 1866 transferred the former Hilton farm property to Reuben Smith for the sum of $1,800. Reuben's son Andrew operated a boardinghouse in the early 20th century, and its brochure boasts a "table furnished from products of the farm" including "berries in season." (Mary Smith Collection.)

This c. 1940 photograph of Orchard Farm taken from the field shows the ell that once connected the house to the barn, with Mary Smith and her older brother Frank standing behind a flock of turkeys. While the ell was later removed, the Cape-style farmhouse and barn still stand on Moultonborough Neck Road, and cattle from the nearby Beede Farm on Schoolhouse Hill graze in the farm fields. (Mary Smith Collection.)

Taken at the Hanson farm on Moultonborough Neck, this c. 1905 photograph shows, from left to right, Charles Hanson, Charles Greene, Dana Hanson, and two unidentified hunters. Brothers Charles and Dana Hanson were the youngest of the six children of Rufus and Mary Hanson. Charles was known for bringing the first Hereford bull to Moultonborough. (Mary Smith Collection.)

Dating to June 1903, this image of a connected farm shows why Moultonborough Neck was described in the 1889 *History of Carroll County* as "purely a farming territory" where "the inhabitants are industrious and thriving farmers, whose profits come from well-cultivated farms, fine herds and flocks, which, with the income from public and private boarding-houses, render them financially independent." (Mary Smith Collection.)

Middle Neck School was at the base of Schoolhouse Hill near the cemetery on Moultonborough Neck Road until 1990, when it was moved to Moultonborough Village and placed next to the Moultonborough Town House. There were three district schools on Moultonborough Neck: Green's Corner, Lower Neck, and Middle Neck. (Mary Smith Collection.)

As shown on the 1892 map, the Smith family had numerous farms on Moultonborough Neck by the early 20th century. This Smith house, where Horace Smith was born in 1844, reportedly burned down after a lightning strike in 1914. Boatman Leander Lavallee, later captain of the *Mount Washington*, stands at far left in this photograph. (Dave Perkins.)

Conceived as a gentleman's country estate, Kona Farm was designed in a Tudor Revival style by Boston architect Harry J. Carlson and built as a summer place for Herbert Dumaresq between 1900 and 1902. The property was listed in the New Hampshire State Register of Historic Places in 2010. (Author's collection.)

Photographer Thomas E. Marr of Boston, known for his images of estate properties, recorded Kona Farm's development from 1900 to 1907. Marr's photographs, shown here as postcards, documented the main house's interior and exterior, as well as the estate's boathouses, barns, and landscaped grounds. (Author's collection.)

Formed by acquiring and then consolidating available farm properties, Kona Farm was recognized as a superior example of the estate-building movement in the early 20th century. This c. 1900 image shows construction of the main house on its hilltop site overlooking Lake Winnipesaukee. (Crowley family.)

This aerial view shows Kona Farm with its principal buildings around 1940. The estate was featured in *New Hampshire Farms for Summer Homes* in 1908 with Thomas E. Marr's photographs of the Tudor Revival residence, boathouses, barns, and associated outbuildings located on about 2,500 acres. (Hare family.)

Described as "a novel boathouse" in the July 1920 issue of *Country Life* magazine, the Swallow Boathouse was designed by Harry J. Carlson and built around 1907 for Herbert Dumaresq's steam yacht *Swallow*, which he acquired in 1905. The Swallow Boathouse was listed in the National Register of Historic Places in 1980.

The Kona Farm livestock barn, originally featuring an E. Howard Company tower clock, was designed to house cows, horses, and poultry, and its plan was published in *Architectural Review* in September 1902. Shown here in a postcard dating to around 1950, the barn later housed Kona Farm Antiques. (Dick Wakefield Collection.)

Originally known as Lake View Farm, this house with its distinctive mansard roof stands at the corner of Ferry Road. Built about 1790 by Daniel Smith as a Cape farmhouse, the structure was expanded around 1870 with a front house in the French Empire style facing Moultonborough Neck Road. (Mary Smith Collection.)

The Lake View post office operated from 1884 until 1908, and this early image, labeled "Dow's house" by the photographer, includes a post office sign. The 1889 *History of Carroll County* notes that "the Neck has a post office, Lake View, formerly kept by Lucien Dow, now by Mrs. Andrew J. Smith." (New Hampshire Historical Society.)

Known locally as the Jim Day house (for its occupants during the early 20th century), Lake View is included in the 1890 state list of boarding establishments with its proprietor noted as J.W. Day. With the ongoing decline of the rural economy that led to farms being abandoned, the house was in a deteriorated state by the 1930s. (Carl Calendar.)

Sue-Louise Calendar bought the former Day house in 1935 for use as a summer place, and it was largely renovated by November of that year. The original Cape farmhouse, which had become the back kitchen ell, as shown above, was removed, and an outdoor terrace was laid in its foundation. (Carl Calendar.)

Starting in the mid-1930s, the Calendar family and visiting friends enjoyed lake and mountain excursions during the summer months. While family albums show some farming activity on the Neck, there are also images of vacant farmhouses. Here, a young Carl Calendar is seated on the bow of the boat. (Carl Calendar.)

This image of the Smith family beach and boathouse was taken around 1910, before Camp Iroquois opened there in 1915. A number of area farm properties were transformed into summer camps for children in the early 20th century. Most of these camps were later sold, and their land was subdivided and developed. (Mary Smith Collection.)

Dr. Ann Tomkins Gibson was the director of Camp Iroquois through 1921, before founding Singing Eagle Lodge on Squam Lake. In an effort to "promote competition in the sports," Iroquois girls were divided into Pine and Birch teams. This image of the Iroquois canoeing teams dates to 1920. (Lake Winnipesaukee Historical Society.)

The Camp Iroquois brochure of 1921 notes that the "camp policy is to take no risks," assuring that "every girl is required to pass a definite swimming test before being allowed in a canoe." Here, war canoes are visible by the camp's bathing beach and boathouse near Salmon Meadow Cove. (Lake Winnipesaukee Historical Society.)

The William Smith farm, midway down Moultonborough Neck on the 1892 map, was located at the foot of Pine Hill and owned by Verna Day Smith in the early 1940s. While William M. Smith was still listed as a farmer in the 1908 *Town Register*, much of his land became part of Kona Farm as area properties were acquired and consolidated to form that country estate property.

Dating to July 1901, this haying scene shows members of area farm families. From left to right atop the hay wagon are Gene Richardson and his mother, Hattie (who later married Alvin Hanson). Standing in front, from left to right, are James Day, Arthur Hanson, Eva Hanson (who later married Cliff Day), two unidentified people, and Alvin Hanson (on the hay rake). (Mary Smith Collection.)

George Washington Smith's Echo Farm, shown here around 1898, was located opposite and just south of Camp Tecumseh. Listed as a farmer in the 1908 *Town Register*, Smith was also a butcher. His farm was demolished around 1919 after it was transferred to James Solomon, who had owned nearby Echo Knoll Farm, the former Edwin Lloyd Smith property, since 1914. (Mary Smith Collection.)

Dating to around 1920, this image shows members of the Day and Hanson families posing with pumpkins at a family gathering. Verna Day and her father, Clifford Day, are in the front. Standing in the rear, from left to right, are Mildred Hood, Eva Hanson Day, Hattie Richardson Hanson, and Alvin Hanson. (Mary Smith Collection.)

This view over the Joseph Smith Farm shows the connected farm prior to its acquisition by Zachary Taylor Hollingsworth in 1901 and subsequent enlargement. The 250-acre Hollingsworth Farm became part of Camp Tecumseh in 1920, allowing for the expansion of the camp's self-sufficient farming operation. (Richardson family.)

The former Hollingsworth Farm remains an integral part of Camp Tecumseh, and it is the only surviving example of a connected farm on Moultonborough Neck. The camp's riding program was active from the 1940s into the 1960s, when sportswoman Abby Belden was the riding instructor. (Camp Tecumseh Archives.)

Camp Tecumseh for boys was established in 1903 on the 100-acre former Town Farm property that had operated there from 1839 until 1898. Dating to 1906, this early photograph shows the c. 1778 Cape farmhouse, now known as the Lodge, and the original livestock barn, now known as the Trunk Room. (Camp Tecumseh Archives.)

This image shows a junior baseball game being played downhill from the Lodge in 1955. While Camp Tecumseh is recognized primarily for its athletics, there is also a drama program, with an annual performance of a Gilbert and Sullivan operetta. The camp's Opera House was built by Buster McCormack in 1960. (Camp Tecumseh Archives.)

Cyrus Davisson, grandfather of Al Davisson, built Trail's End opposite Long Point in 1923. It is one of the earliest cottages in the Far Echoes Colony and remains in the Davisson family today. With its rustic porch and setting among the trees, the property retains great integrity as a surviving example of an early 20th century lake cottage. (Mark Dodd.)

Davisson family albums show decades of camp life and recreation on Lake Winnipesaukee, with boating, fishing, and other area excursions. Al Davisson summered at Trail's End all his life, going between the family cottage and Davisson Farm on Moultonborough Neck Road. (Mark Dodd.)

George "Spinach" Greene was the agent for the Lake Company and frequented the growing Far Echoes Colony to provide services in his steamboat the *West Wind*, shown here in 1921. The caption identifies the "launch that takes us to market—six miles down the lake to Weirs and Laconia." (Robert Girouard.)

A number of seasonal cottages were constructed on Lake Company lots along the shoreline of the George Smith farm in the early 20th century in what became known as the Far Echoes Colony. The Scobey (later Carvell) cottage called Pebble Beach was built in 1911 and badly damaged in the hurricane of 1938. (Mary Smith Collection.)

Originally operated by Lynde Eleazer Davis out of one end of his barn, the L.E. Davis store expanded over time to offer gas, rental cottages, miniature golf, and movies, which were shown in the field across the road by the Davis farmhouse. This c. 1938 photograph shows Ada (second from left) and Lynde Davis (far right) with two of their many grandchildren.

The L.E. Davis store was acquired by Davis grandson Leroy (Buster) McCormack and his wife, Doris, in 1944, when it was expanded and became known as McCormack's Store. The McCormacks ran the store until 1973, and it became JoJo's Country Store in 1977, with a new building erected in 1988. (McCormack family.)

Five

LOWER NECK AND LONG ISLAND

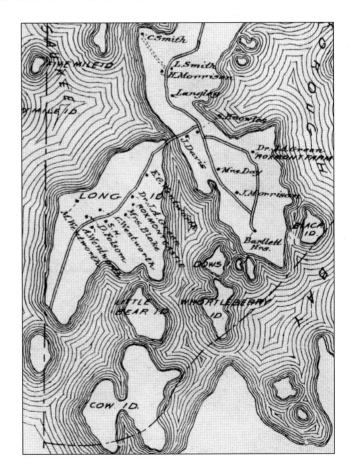

This detail showing
Moultonborough Lower
Neck and Long Island is
taken from D.H. Hurd's
1892 *Town and City Atlas of
the State of New Hampshire.*

Prior to the influx of tourism in the 1880s and the building of summer homes, Moultonborough's Lower Neck was primarily farmland worked by early families. This mid-1930s photograph shows the historic Langdon farmhouse, called the Bouerie when it was owned by the Hulse family as a summer home, at the head of what is now known as Langdon Cove. (Calendar family.)

Dr. Jared Alonzo Greene established the Roxmont Poultry Farm on the Lower Neck in 1890. Originally consisting of 1,300 acres, his estate farm featured modern incubator and poultry buildings and boasted an annual production of 120,000 chickens and ducks. Greene's steamboat *Roxmont* transported produce to his New Hotel Weirs and other destinations on the lake. (Laconia Library.)

Dr. J.A. Greene's estate farm barn was transformed into the Winnipesaukee Inn in 1907. Here, a team of carpenters led by master builder Perley Hall is shown at the construction site. Hall married George Washington Smith's daughter Lida from Echo Farm on Moultonborough Neck that same year. This image was provided by Lida's great-granddaughter. (Theresa Perrin.)

The Winnipesaukee Inn, conceived as the family-style counterpart to Dr. J.A. Greene's New Hotel Weirs, was in operation from 1907 to about 1919. The property was sold to the International Sunday School Association in 1919, which then established Geneva Point Camp (now Geneva Point Center) at the site. (Dick Wakefield Collection.)

In August 1890, a group of Bates College graduates from the class of 1879 acquired Wentworth Point from Dr. J.A. Greene for $100 and built a rustic fishing camp in 1891. What became known as Camp '79 (or the Red Camp) survives there today. Over time, summer cottages for the Given, Johonnot, Ranger, and Tuttle families were established on what was by then called Garnet Point (for the Bates College colors). (Given family.)

Dr. Emery W. Given built Camp Rest Awhile on Garnet Point in 1899. Lines from John Greenleaf Whittier's 1853 poem "Summer by the Lakeside: Lake Winnipesaukee" were inscribed on a board mounted over the fireplace, as shown here around 1900. Given was included in the list of seasonal residents published in the 1904 edition of *New Hampshire Farms for Summer Homes*, and his descendants summered at Camp Rest Awhile until 2016, when the property was sold, and the house was demolished. (Given family.)

The Camp '79 property's landing, shown above with figures, was located on the former Wentworth Point. A number of images in the Given family albums show Garnet Point prior to any development, when just the Red Camp was located there. (Given family.)

Camp Rest Awhile's original boathouse on Langdon Cove, shown here in 1911 with a new porch, was later used as a bunkhouse and has since been demolished. This image shows Winifred Given at left in a dory on the boat ramp with her mother, Helen, at right. (Given family.)

Dr. Emery W. Given's 28-foot motorboat *Bluebird* was said to be the second-fastest boat on the lake. While *Bluebird* was destroyed in a fire, his Rushton guide boat, now owned by his great-grandson Keith Given, can still be seen on Lake Winnipesaukee. (Given family.)

A new boathouse was built for the *Bluebird* in 1911. The large upstairs room was used for many years for neighborhood gatherings, hymn sings, and church services by the Camp '79 group and the greater Langdon Cove community. (Given family.)

Geneva Point Camp, also known as Geneva Point International Training Schools in its early years, was established on the former Winnipesaukee Inn property in 1919. Many campers and visitors arrived by steamboat, as shown in this photograph of the *Governor Endicott* docking at the camp's landing in the 1920s. (Geneva Point Center Archives.)

Existing Roxmont Poultry Farm and Winnipesaukee Inn buildings, including a barn, were moved and renovated for camp uses over time. New buildings, including the monumental chapel (dedicated in 1930), were also added to the Geneva Point Camp property, as shown in this aerial view of the campus. (Geneva Point Center Archives.)

Camp Robindel was established in 1951 by educators Paddy and Adele Feldman in collaboration with Eli and Fanny Robinson, owners of the popular Robinson's Lodge resort property near Geneva Point in the 1940s. Under new ownership since 2021, this beloved camp for girls is still in operation today. (Camp Robindel.)

Original buildings from the Robinson's Lodge era, including the open-air playhouse, are still in use at Camp Robindel. Aside from enjoying sports and other activities on Langdon Cove, campers take part in longstanding traditions such as Friday Shabbat dinner, which features freshly baked challah bread. (Camp Robindel.)

The Plumfield Camp for Girls, open from 1939 to 1981, was established by Mary Rose Hilton and later run by her daughter Jean, whose brother Ted operated the Deer Hill Camp for Boys. Jean Hilton was the longtime director of the Plumfield School in Darien, Connecticut, which was founded by her mother. (Hilton family.)

Plumfield Camp was known for its riding program in addition to traditional activities and water sports. The camp's farmhouse and barn still stand across from one another on Winaukee Road, although the 60-acre property and its Dow Island acreage was sold in 1986 and subsequently developed. (Hilton family.)

Founded in 1920, Camp Winaukee for Boys features a mainland campus and a Black Island camp for teenagers, which opened in 1946. This image shows the camp's historic farmhouse in 1948. Camp Winaukee directors Jesse "Doc" Sobel and Moe Spahn brought a focus on sports to the camp in the 1930s. (Camp Winaukee.)

Camp Winaukee's arts and crafts program was led by art director Paul Repasy, whose work appears in many buildings and sites on the campus, including the Playhouse, shown here in 1950. Leonard Plaisted is remembered as the man who built most of the camp's buildings starting in 1924. (Camp Winaukee.)

Boris Witte started Witte's Boats and Motors in 1946, and he and his wife, Eva, opened Witte's Store near the Long Island Bridge in 1947, where they sold gas, boating and fishing supplies, and ice cream. The business was sold to William Prince in 1952, expanded by Don Ross in the 1960s, and acquired by the Trexler family in 1972. Dick Wakefield designed the lighthouse built on the dock in 1976. (Trexler's Marina.)

Abby Snow Belden, a cigar-smoking Smith College graduate, was the director of Camp Winnicut for Girls on 200 acres near Morrison Cove from the mid-1920s into the 1930s. Belden's excursion boat is shown here with the camp's boathouse in the background. After the steamboat was acquired by Charles E. George in 1937, it was renamed the *Anna E.*, after his wife, and depicted on Moultonborough's town seal painted by Ernest Davis. (David Thompson.)

This photograph of the Long Island Bridge dates to around 1900. According to Frances Stevens's *As I Remember Moultonborough*, published in 1987, a barge pulled by her father Charles E. George's boat transported cars between Moultonborough Neck and Long Island when the bridge was being rebuilt in October 1935. (Tuftonboro Historical Society.)

This image shows Stewart Dow playing with his toy boat with the Long Island Bridge in the background in the summer of 1929. The Dow house on Moultonborough Neck, built by David Dow in 1814, is recognized as one of the oldest houses in the area. The property is still owned by Dow descendants. (Adam Ricker.)

Dr. Jared Alonzo Greene built his summer residence, Roxmont (shown here under construction in 1890), on a 40-acre parcel he acquired in 1889 at the high point of Long Island. Images of Roxmont, also known as Greene's Castle, were published in the *Granite Monthly* in January 1896. Roxmont burned down in 1932, but stone pillars still mark the estate's former entrance on Long Island Road.

Period accounts of Dr. J.A. Greene's Roxmont describe the property's plantings and landscaped grounds, as shown here with a figure standing by the reflecting pond along the driveway leading to the front of the house. Roxmont's interior was known for Greene's art collection, fine furnishings, and the objects collected by the Greenes during their world travels. (Austin family.)

Dr. Frank Eugene Greene's summer estate Windermere, designed by Boston architect J.H. Besarick, was built in the Queen Anne style at the tip of Long Island in 1891–1892 on the site of the former Robert Lamprey farm. Conceived as a gentleman's self-sustaining property with a double barn and caretaker's cottage, Windermere was listed in the National Register of Historic Places in 1979.

Windermere's original boathouse burned down in 1906. Flora Greene Armstrong, sister of brothers J.A. and F.E. Greene of Moultonborough, summered with her husband, George, at the Gilnockie estate in nearby Center Harbor, where their *Gilnockie* is shown here at its dock. Summer residents enjoyed lake excursions and water carnivals at the Weirs. (Lake Winnipesaukee Historical Society.)

Known locally as Blake's Hotel and situated at the crest of Long Island adjacent to Greene's Roxmont, the Island Home was operated by Levi Blake in the 1890s, during the heyday of boardinghouse tourism. The Island Home is included in the 1890 list of boarding establishments and listed in Frank West Rollins's *The Tourists' Guide-Book to the State of New Hampshire* (1902).

An 1878 advertisement for the Island Home, when it was initially operated by proprietors Blake and Lamprey, advises that guests traveling by rail could reach the Island Home via the steamboats *Mount Washington* or *Lady of the Lake*, which would arrive at the Long Island Landing. The long-vacant hotel building burned down in October 1962.

Established as the Long Island House by George K. Brown in 1874 and operated by successive generations, this property could accommodate up to 50 guests by 1900. Brown's hotel is included in the 1890 state list of boarding establishments and listed in Frank West Rollins's *The Tourists' Guide-Book to the State of New Hampshire* (1902). (Austin family.)

Family photographs show how the John Brown homestead, built in 1821, was expanded by his son George K. Brown over decades to add a dining room and additional guest rooms. An annex was added to the property around 1900. The Long Island Inn was listed in the New Hampshire State Register of Historic Places in 2010. (Austin family.)

Long Island Inn is a prime example of early tourism and the boardinghouse era in Moultonborough. Housing the Long Island post office from 1878 to 1917 and situated at a major port, the Brown family's establishment flourished into the 20th century and is still owned by Brown family descendants. (Austin family.)

The tree-lined lane to Long Island Landing went straight down to the lake from the front door of the hotel, which was known as the Long Island Inn from around 1911. Images from family albums show the Model A beach wagon that was used to transport guests and luggage from the wharf up to the inn. (Austin family.)

Long Island Landing, also known as Brown's Wharf, was Moultonborough's principal port on Lake Winnipesaukee in the early 20th century. Period brochures for tourist excursion boats, such as the *Gracie* (shown here) or the mailboat *Uncle Sam*, advertise day trips to destinations all around the lake. (Austin family.)

This 1880s photograph shows the *Mount Washington* and the *Lamprey* at a bustling Long Island Landing. While the Long Island freight house, built around 1900, is no longer standing, the basin at the left of the image still marks the former site of the wharf. (Lake Winnipesaukee Historical Society.)

Back Bay was popular with guests staying at Long Island's boarding establishments, as shown here. M.F. Sweetser's *White Mountains: Handbook for Travellers* (1888) notes: "There are pleasant groves and beaches on the island, and conveniences for boating, bathing, fishing, hunting and riding." (Austin family.)

The Long Island Inn's laundry house was located at Back Bay's sheltered cove. Island families were known for their boatmen, and this image shows Capt. Herbert A. Blackstone's *Maid of the Isles* at Back Bay before rebuilding. Blackstone was married to George K. Brown's daughter Malvina. (Austin family.)

Six

EAST SIDE

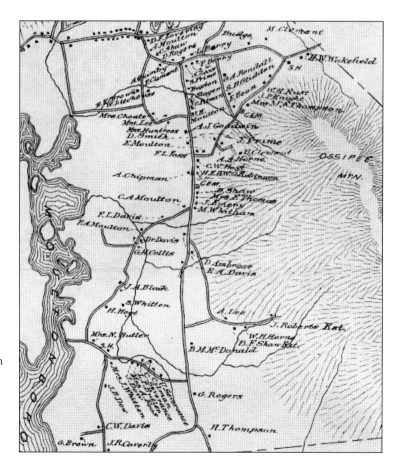

This detail showing East Moultonborough with the Ossipee Mountains is taken from D.H. Hurd's 1892 *Town and City Atlas of the State of New Hampshire.*

This photograph shows Will Raymond's boat *Beatrice* at Lee's Mills with the Ossipee Mountains in the background. Lee's Mills was a headquarters for logging at the turn of the 20th century, and as many as 75 men were employed by the lumber-related industries located there. (Lively family.)

This image, featuring a barge loaded with lumber, shows what was once a common sight at Lee's Mills and other landings around Lake Winnipesaukee when sawmills, shingle mills, and other early industries were still active. In the mid-19th century, Lee's Mills was also a landing for the passenger steamer *Red Hill*. (Dave Perkins.)

Winifred Given, whose family summered at Garnet Point on the Lower Neck, is shown here on a log raft in Green's Basin in 1919. Contemporary accounts report how children "snaked" or rode the logs near mill sites. Green's Basin was a popular place for boating in summer and ice fishing in winter. (Given family.)

Lee's Mills is the best known of Moultonborough's early industrial sites. After building a dam to impound Lower Pond (now known as Lee's Pond), David Lee built a sawmill in the early 19th century. In 1887, it was acquired by Isaac Adams, who expanded operations. This image shows the Adams Mill after the washout of 1895.

Owned by the same family since the early 20th century, Catnip Lodge is a landmark property on Lee's Mills Road. George Fales bought the former McKeen land and buildings from Harry Blanchard in 1906, adding extensive gardens over time. Family albums show well-dressed summer guests enjoying Catnip Lodge and its grounds and recreational boating on Lake Winnipesaukee. (Bob Knell.)

While Lou Fales appears in pictures taken at his brother George's Catnip Lodge, he also owned a property off Ferry Road on Moultonborough Neck. This photograph, printed from a glass negative, shows his steamboat *The Lynn*. As seen in the 1942 real estate assessment list, Louis Wyman later owned the former Louis Fales place of 85 acres at Lovejoy Point, at that time valued at $7,500.

Peter and Mildred Carter Larson bought Homestead Farm in 1929 and made numerous improvements while expanding farm operations in the 1930s and 1940s. In this image, Peter O. Larson is walking down the farm's driveway with the brick house and barn in the background. The bricks used to build the original Lyman Brown farmhouse were fabricated on the property. (Lively family.)

Homestead Farm, shown in this aerial view, was known for its apple production in the 1940s. Peter and Mildred Carter Larson planted an apple orchard with about 100 trees in the 1930s and rebuilt an old dam in 1940 for irrigation. A large poultry barn was added around 1950. Located on Lee Road (and now known as the Old Orchard Inn), the property still retains a section of the Larsons' apple orchard.

This 1914 image shows Camp Inwood, the red cottage on Whaleback Point that can be seen by boaters departing from the Lee's Mills boat launch. Acquired by Willis and Myra Brown Carter in 1912, Camp Inwood has been the retreat of the Lively family (who are Brown family descendants) since 1958. (Lively family.)

Many of the early camps in the area were accessed by boats kept at Lee's Mills, as shown in this image from the Fales family albums. Summer camp owners kept oars in marked storage areas in the barn at Homestead Farm on Lee Road, where they could also pick up mail, produce, and other supplies. (Bob Knell.)

Harry Blanchard transferred Little Pine Island, along with its buildings, to Arthur and Perne Brown Weeks in October 1906. The island camp was called Camp Itsuitsus in the whimsical fashion of other nearby summer cottages, including October Morn, October Eve, Gray Gull, Seldom Inn, and Rest Haven. (Lively family.)

Will Carter's boat *Weonit* is shown in this 1914 photograph, with Camp Itsuitsus visible on Little Pine Island in the background. Will Carter is at the helm, Arthur and Perne Weeks are seated in the stern, and their daughter Maxine is standing near the bow. (Lively family.)

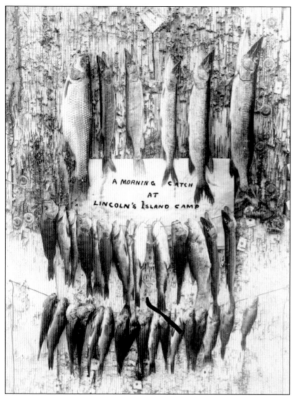

A MORNING CATCH
AT
LINCOLN'S ISLAND CAMP

Edward C. Lincoln acquired what are now known as the Lincoln Islands from Harry Blanchard in 1907. Around 1910, Edward and his wife, Violet, built rustic camp lodges that were rented to vacationers on a weekly basis from mid-May until Labor Day. Fishing was one of the main attractions. Guests at Lincoln's Island Camp enjoyed simply furnished cabins with lake views and "catch of the day" dinners cooked by Violet, which were described as featuring "good plain food and plenty of it" in the printed brochure. The rate was $10 per week, including meals and use of the camp rowboats, as shown in the below image. (Lincoln family.)

The island cabins, which measured 10 feet by 10 feet and were built from log slabs and birchbark, were similar to other primitive shanties built in the early 20th century for visitors seeking to experience the wilderness. The Lincoln's Island Camp dock was located at Cozy Island, shown below around 1915 with a low water level in Lake Winnipesaukee. The camp enterprise operated until about 1921. All of the cabins and trees on the island were destroyed by fire in 1937. Successive generations of the Lincoln family built cabins and continue to spend time on the Lincoln Islands. (Lincoln family.)

Known as the Goss house, this Cape farmhouse stands at the corner of Bodge Hill Road and Governor Wentworth Highway. Edgar Goss, who served as town clerk, is listed as a farmer and carpenter in the 1908 census. The property has been in the Wakefield family since 1945. The Goss Corner School, indicated on both the 1861 and 1892 town maps, was located just north of it.

Horace Smith acquired the John Slager house, known as the Elms, in 1907. In 1908, Smith moved a large barn and woodshed from across the road to create a connected farm compound. Horace and Ernestine Richardson moved to the property in 1927, and Horace's aunt Ethel Smith, longtime schoolteacher and town clerk, continued to reside there. This property, with its restored barn and prominent silo, is now known as the Davis Farm.

The John Moulton homestead, built in the mid-1700s by one of the town's original grantees, was occupied by generations of Moultons until it was acquired by Lyman Francis Blake in 1931. This Cape farmhouse, with its central chimney, appears on the 1861 and 1892 maps and is located on Governor Wentworth Highway directly across from Lee Road. (Hazel Gray.)

Harold and Minnie Gordon bought the historic John Moulton farm in 1933. Harold was a carpenter in the 1930s and 1940s while he continued to farm his property, as shown in numerous family photographs in the possession of his granddaughter Hazel Gray. He was also an accomplished artist, and his paintings of area places are in local collections. (Hazel Gray.)

Ernest E. Davis bought the Charles Hoyt farm in 1904. He opened a boarding establishment called Pleasantdale House in 1910, and it operated until his wife, Ellen, passed away in 1922. The property accommodated 20 guests and was known for lodging vaudeville entertainers and opera singers, according to its last family occupant, Ernest E. Davis Jr., who is remembered as a longtime selectman, Grange member, and historian.

Boarders enjoyed "delightful mountain views" and were close to Ossipee Mountain Park and other summer destinations. Guests of the William Plant family, whose property (known as Tanglewood) was on Tuftonboro Neck, stayed at Pleasantdale in 1912 at the time of a family wedding. Pleasantdale House was in a deteriorated state by 2000, then restored to its original appearance by Paul Lacaillade from 2005 to 2007.

This October 1912 photograph of William Plant's sons on a hunting trip was taken at Prospect Cottage, one of the larger boardinghouses of its time. In *The Tourists' Guide-Book to the State of New Hampshire* (1902), this "enlarged and newly furnished" property is described as "beautifully located on one of the foothills of Ossipee Mountain, near Lake Winnipiseogee and Ossipee Mountain Park. Views of lake and mountain unexcelled." (Plant family.)

William Robinson's Prospect Cottage, shown here with boarders on the side porch, accommodated 30 guests at $1 per day or $5 to $7 per week year-round. *The Tourists' Guide-Book to the State of New Hampshire* (1902) notes how "excellent trout and bass fishing makes it a desirable resort for fishermen both summer and winter." Robinson also operated the livery stable for Ossipee Mountain Park from his property, offering drives and excursions "at reasonable prices."

The Crow's Nest pavilion was a highlight for visitors to Ossipee Mountain Park, and the 1908 *Town Register* notes: "The climb to Ossipee Mountain makes the trip to the park complete, from this vantage point one of the best views to be obtained in the state is found." Period postcards of the Crow's Nest abound, with some of them showing graffiti covering the structure. (Leach family.)

Tourists flocked to Ossipee Mountain Park to enjoy the natural wonders described by Lucy Larcom's article "In the Ossipee Glens," published in *New England Magazine* in 1892. Visitors also experienced the rural picturesque that attracted artists when viewing the vacant farmhouses of the Lee Settlement, which had largely been abandoned by the time of the park's opening in 1880. (Oliver family.)

A stop at Ossipee Falls (now known as the Falls of Song), a spectacular feature along Shannon Brook, was often a highlight for Ossipee Mountain Park visitors. As noted in the 1908 *Town Register*, "a comfortable path leads you to the cascade and rustic bridges cross the brook in many places." Period images show tourists at popular sites along the Brook Walk, including Whittier Falls and the Bridal Veil. (Author's collection.)

Benjamin Franklin Shaw acquired land in the Lee Settlement in 1879, building Weelahka Hall in the valley below the Crow's Nest (shown at top left) to accommodate guests and developing Ossipee Mountain Park. Black Snout was renamed Mount Shaw in his honor on the Fourth of July in 1884. The park was described as the town's "principal attraction" and "mecca for hundreds of coaching parties from miles around" in the 1908 *Town Register*. (Dick Wakefield Collection.)

The Lee Homestead was located at the top of the town road leading to the early settlement in the Ossipee Mountains (now Ossipee Park Road), as shown on the 1861 and 1892 maps of the area. Five generations of the Lee family lived and farmed on the mountain until 1913, when Thomas G. Plant acquired their family property, and the Lees relocated to Sheridan Road. (Oliver family.)

This photograph shows Shaw family members atop Lee Mountain, with a view over the principal buildings of Ossipee Mountain Park in the valley below, and open fields visible on the slopes of Mount Roberts. The Lee farm is at left along the tree-lined roadway, Shaw's Weelahka Hall is to the right, and the park's large barn with a cupola is at the center of the image. (Oliver family.)

Thomas G. Plant bought Ossipee Mountain Park in 1911, and the property became the centerpiece of his country estate. Encountering resistance from the Lee family as he continued to acquire and consolidate area properties, Plant built what was called a spite fence to block their view, a move covered by the *Boston Globe* and other newspapers in 1912. (Oliver family.)

This October 1912 photograph shows members of the Plant family driving past the former barn and spite fence at Ossipee Mountain Park after a visit to see Thomas G. Plant's recently acquired property. Other photographs from the family albums show stops at the Crow's Nest pavilion and the famous waterfalls on the park property. (Plant family.)

Designed by J. Williams Beal & Sons, Architects of Boston, Thomas G. Plant's "country house" was built in 1914 and published with its floor plans in the April 1924 issue of *Country Life* magazine. Shown here under construction in 1914, this Arts and Crafts–style house, which Plant and his wife, Olive, called Lucknow, was intended to blend into its mountaintop surroundings. (Plant family.)

Shown here from Sunset Hill, Thomas G. Plant's Lucknow was built on the former site of the Crow's Nest viewing pavilion. Having lost his fortune, Plant attempted to sell the estate with an 18-page advertisement in the October 1924 issue of *Country Life* magazine. Now known as the Castle in the Clouds, this landmark property was listed in the National Register of Historic Places in 2018. (Tuftonboro Historical Society.)

Aside from the main house, combination stable and garage, and other outbuildings including a boathouse on Lake Winnipesaukee, Thomas G. Plant's Lucknow estate featured boundary walls and two stone gate lodges at the entrances to the property. This postcard shows the lower gate with the Brook Lodge, which is the principal estate entrance located on Old Mountain Road. (Dick Wakefield Collection.)

Lucknow, Thomas G. Plant's estate, was photographed by George Wesley Perry, whose images were reproduced as postcards, used in publicity, and included in sales brochures and advertisements for the estate starting in the 1920s. This Perry photograph shows the large gambrel combination barn and dwelling at the Plant farm, now known as Ledgewood Farm. (New Hampshire Historical Society.)

The McDonald family operated the Mineral Spring House as a seasonal boarding establishment near Ossipee Mountain Park, catering to tourists coming to take "the cure" at a nearby mineral spring. Described as "An ideal spot for any one to spend a vacation for rest and recreation" in *The Tourists' Guide-Book to the State of New Hampshire* (1902), the property accommodated 15 guests at $1 per day, or $5 to $7 per week. (Author's collection.)

This c. 1880 view of the McDonald property shows the connected farm barns removed by Thomas G. Plant after he bought the property in 1913, while amassing acreage for his country estate. Plant substantially renovated the house in the 1920s when developing his Bald Peak Country Club, renaming it Westwynde. (Author's collection.)

Cesare and Josephine Vappi bought Westwynde as a summer place for their family in 1941, acquiring additional acreage in the valley as Thomas G. Plant's Lucknow estate was subdivided and sold off after his death that year. Taken at Westwynde in 1950, this photograph shows Cesare at far right and his son Richard standing at center, along with two unidentified bear hunters. (Author's collection.)

Richard Vappi, a graduate of the Thompson School of Agriculture at the University of New Hampshire, established Westwynde Farm on the family property with his wife, Jean. This large gambrel dairy barn (for the herd of Holstein cows), poultry barn, and other agricultural outbuildings were constructed in 1950. (Author's collection.)

Mrs. George W. Gilman's seasonal Sunset Cottage on what is now Severance Road accommodated 12 guests at $1 per day. Frank West Rollins's *The Tourists' Guide-Book to the State of New Hampshire* (1902) described it as a "comfortable and neat-appearing house with spacious, well-lighted, and well-ventilated rooms . . . located on high and dry land about midway between Ossipee Mountain Park and Lake Winnipiseogee." (Burrows family.)

Rollins also noted how Sunset Cottage "has [a] piazza on south and west sides and commands magnificent and widespread mountain and intervale views" and also offered "unsurpassed opportunities for brook and lake fishing." Guests could enjoy views from the summerhouse or lodge on the property, which still stands across Severance Road from the main house. (Burrows family.)

Home of Col. Jonathan Moulton's foster son Bradbury Richardson, this early homestead was built around 1770. The property is located in the fertile valley near Shannon Brook. When early generations of the Richardson family populated this area, the district school formerly at the end of today's Severance Road was known as the Richardson School. (David Severance.)

One of Richardson's granddaughters married Samuel Severance, and the property remains in the Severance family today. The house was occupied by Charles Severance by the time of the 1892 town map and by William Severance and his wife, Grace, by the 1920s. This image shows the updated farm property with an enclosed porch, portico entrance, blinds and striped awnings. (David Severance.)

Thomas G. Plant's boathouse for his Lucknow country estate was located on Lake Winnipesaukee at what is now known as Ambrose Cove. In Plant's time, the boathouse was accessed through internal estate roads. This unusual view shows an open porch structure and pier attached to the main boathouse. The buildings were reportedly demolished by the 1950s. (Lincoln family.)

Howard Arey opened Arey's Marina with the Lakeside Superette around 1960, and his emporium quickly became a destination for boaters and neighbors in the Moultonborough Bay area. Later, under the ownership of Andy and Pat Anderson, the property featured a snack bar and was renamed Ambrose Cove Marina. Today, it is a large boat storage and valet boat slip operation. (Author's collection.)

After building his Lucknow estate, Thomas G. Plant planned and developed a residential country club on the shores of Lake Winnipesaukee. The Boston architectural firm of Haven & Hoyt designed the row of Arts and Crafts–style cottages built on the ridge in 1919 and 1920. The cottages all featured sleeping porches facing the Ossipee Mountains and verandas with lake views. (Author's collection.)

Designed by Chase Roy Whitcher, New Hampshire's first state architect, the Bald Peak clubhouse is representative of period country club architecture with its dining rooms, entertainment spaces, changing rooms, and accommodations for visitors. Known as the Bald Peak Colony Club since 1932, the club features a golf course designed by Donald Ross and mountain and lake views. (Author's collection.)

DISCOVER THOUSANDS OF LOCAL HISTORY BOOKS FEATURING MILLIONS OF VINTAGE IMAGES

Arcadia Publishing, the leading local history publisher in the United States, is committed to making history accessible and meaningful through publishing books that celebrate and preserve the heritage of America's people and places.

Find more books like this at
www.arcadiapublishing.com

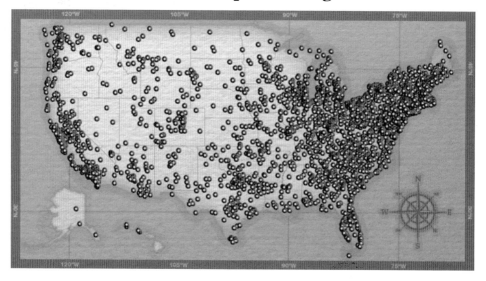

Search for your hometown history, your old stomping grounds, and even your favorite sports team.

Consistent with our mission to preserve history on a local level, this book was printed in South Carolina on American-made paper and manufactured entirely in the United States. Products carrying the accredited Forest Stewardship Council (FSC) label are printed on 100 percent FSC-certified paper.

MADE IN THE USA